Serenity Garden

7 Radical Weeds for Natural Stress Relief

Cultivate Inner Peace

California Poppy · Catnip · Chamomile
Lavender · Lemon Balm · Skullcap · Valerian

A GARDEN REMEDY BOOK WITH FREE SEEDS BY

Jillian VanNostrand & Christie V. Sarles

ILLUSTRATIONS BY

Martha Gail Copplestone

With love
to our family and friends
for their cultivation of Radical Weeds
&
with heartfelt gratitude to Susun Weed
who helps us to say what we really mean

SIMPLE BOOKS WITH FREE, FRESH SEEDS
There's a garden in every one...everyone into the garden!

Published by Radical Weeds
P.O. Box 68, Mirror Lake, NH 03853-0068
Copyright ©1999 by Jillian VanNostrand and Christie V. Sarles
All rights reserved.

ISBN 0-9664246-1-1

Book design by Todd Smith / Design

Only you have the power to take responsibility for all of your
health care decisions. Consult your own inner wisdom, and
check with your health practitioner and herbalist for guidance
in making informed choices about your own unique body in
relation to any of the contents of this book.
No guarantees.

Table of Contents

1
Step Into Our Garden

2
Serenity Garden

5
California Poppy

7
Catnip

9
Chamomile

11
Lavender

13
Lemon Balm

15
Skullcap

17
Valerian

18
Starting Seeds Indoors & Out

21
Harvesting & Storing Plants & Seeds

22
Making Plant Remedies
*Teas, Water & Oil Infusions, Tinctures, Steam Facials,
Herbal Baths, Salt Glows, Salves, Capsules*

26
Additional Resources
Books & Supplies

27
Postcard for Free Seeds

Postcard for Radical Weeds

Step into our garden...

We two sisters have worked with radical weeds for more than 30 years. We've grown and used them for ourselves, our families, and our friends, for a midwifery practice, for two herbal mail order businesses, and for countless workshops and weed walks. We invite you to share our homegrown wisdom, and to pass some seeds along. Help to spread the bounty of radical weeds into many lives and places!

By "radical weed," we mean any plant that you can cultivate and use to help strengthen your well-being. Radical means root, and the use of plants is the oldest, deepest root of medicine. It runs from past to present in healing traditions and practices the Earth over. Knowledge of plant medicine is ancient and powerful. It has not always come easily or without cost. Sowing the seeds of radical weeds and spreading this knowledge into the future serves Earth's well-being and your own profoundly and directly: radically.

The remedies you make from plants you have grown from seed are radical medicine for whole health that resonate with your natural will to mend. Growing, making, and using your own vital remedies is a down to Earth choice whose time has come — again. Send for your seeds, and use this simple book as your guide to a powerful harvest.

Jillian & Christie

Serenity Garden

Gardeners benefit from cultivation, too.

Earth's vital force flows into you every time you work a garden. Cultivate, and your garden cultivates you back, recharging and reweaving your whole being. Gardening taps a deep well of serenity in the gardener. And the benefits don't stop at the garden's edge. Long after the growing season, the harvest from your Serenity Garden will continue to nourish and strengthen you.

Stress is part of life, and all of us live with it daily, from the cranky infant to the tense commuter to the sleepless elder to the grieving partner. Even normal and necessary everyday actions like eating and exercise unavoidably produce stress. Our bodies are built to handle all kinds of stress — nutritional, physical, emotional, spiritual, environmental — but unrelieved stress of any kind takes a heavy toll on all body systems. The ability to resolve stress without becoming ill depends largely on the strength of the entire nervous system. To stay healthy we must heed the warning signals and take care to nourish, rest, and replenish ourselves.

Feeling sluggish and depressed, or wired, anxious and irritable, or having trouble sleeping are all signs of nervous system overload. Other warning signals include digestive disturbances like indigestion, colic, irritable bowel, and sometimes ulcers. You can use radical weeds to help manage these problems safely and effectively. Regular use can even increase your body's natural tolerance for stress, right down to the cellular level.

The seven radical weeds in your Serenity Garden provide vital nutrients, especially minerals, for maintaining strong, sound nerves. They work gently yet powerfully to calm anxiety, relieve tension, ease headaches and heartaches, resolve nervous indigestion, relax muscle spasms, promote restful sleep, and generally give you a break from stress-related symptoms, without side effects.

While your garden grows, you can reduce the effects of stress in other ways. Eat more whole grains. Have oatmeal for breakfast. Snack on seaweed. Reduce your intake of caffeine, alcohol, tobacco, and refined sugar. Stretch out every day. Take a hot bath. Walk more. Dance more. Sing more. Touch more.

Enhance your Serenity Garden remedies by using the elements with imagination. Heat relaxes even the most resistant muscles. The simple sound of running water can induce a healing trance. Earth offers many treasures to energize and ground you, beginning with the dirt under your bare feet. And ahhhh, air....

Breathe deeply often. Take a slow, deep breath through your nose, then let it all out on a great big open-mouthed, out-loud Ahhhhhhhhhhhhh. If you end up yawning, so much the better. Deep breathing floods the nerves with oxygen and helps you to relax. Take another breath, and another. Inhale all the healing scents of your garden. Cultivate inner peace. Serenity awaits you....

California Poppy

Eschscholzia californica, Cup of Gold

California Poppy has a mild sedative and pain-relieving action that calms anxiety and promotes restful sleep. West coast Native Americans have long used it to soothe colicky babies, and in Europe it's used to calm hyperactive children. For adults, California Poppy's nerve-strengthening properties make it an effective remedy for occasional insomnia, stress headaches, and nervous facial tics. This is not an opium Poppy.

Uses

- Nourishes & strengthens nerves
- Calms anxiety
- Eases tension headaches
- Induces restful sleep without hangover
- Relaxes muscle spasms, cramps, tics

Cultivation

Long ago, ships off the California coast navigated by sighting on distant hillsides covered with the bright orange flowers of California Poppy. Now legally protected in its native habitat, it grows easily from seed sown directly outside in a sunny, sandy spot. (See page 19.) Plants reach 12-18" tall with grey-green, feathery leaves and delicate, orangey-gold flowers that bloom all summer, closing up at night and on overcast days. Harvest the whole plant in full bloom — roots and all. Be sure to leave some plants to go to seed.

Preparation

Use the whole plant, fresh or dried, for teas or tinctures. Take the tea for mild symptoms and the tincture when you require stronger relief. You can smoke a pipe of the dried plant for mild relaxation.

California Poppy Tea *

For a cup of tea, pour boiling water over a teaspoon of dried herb (double the amount if fresh) and steep for at least 10 minutes. Enjoy freely! For a stronger water-based remedy than tea, make an infusion. (See page 22.)

California Poppy Tincture **

Pack a clean, dry jar with fresh California Poppy, including roots. Pour in all-natural brandy or any 80 proof vodka to cover completely. Cover, label, date, and store away from heat or light for six weeks. Strain into a measuring cup, then pour into dark glass dropper bottles. Label and date. Take 1-2 droppersful up to 3 times a day, as needed.

*More about teas on page 22. **More about tinctures, including an alcohol-free version, on page 23.

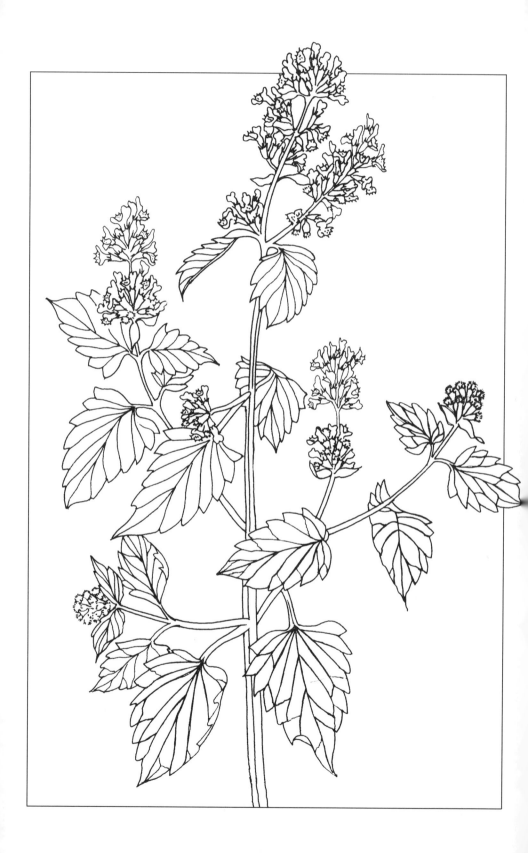

Catnip

Nepeta cataria, Catswort

Like all Mints, Catnip is a nervine and muscle relaxant. It relieves digestive and emotional distress by easing muscle spasms, eliminating gas, and balancing blood sugar. Catnip is a mood stabilizer rich in B vitamins, and it makes a favorite remedy for women with PMS or menstrual cramps. Catnip tea can soothe both a tired mother and — through her milk — her infant, too. Catnip is also useful for treating hyperactive children, as it helps them to focus.

Uses

- Nourishes & strengthens nerves
- Relaxes muscle spasms, relieves menstrual cramps
- Soothes digestive upsets, alleviates gas
- Calms anxiety
- Induces restful sleep without hangover

Cultivation

Catnip thrives in full sun and poor, acidic soil. Bees love it. So do cats, of course. An old saying goes, "If you set it, cats'll get it, but if you sow it, they won't know it," and it does seem to go longer undetected by cats when you start it from seed outside. Catnip can grow over 3' tall, with grey-green leaves and tiny white flowers. Harvest the top third of the plant just before it blooms. Use fresh for maximum potency.

Preparation

Use fresh whenever possible for teas and tinctures. You can smoke a pipe of dried Catnip for quick relief from menstrual cramps.

Catnip Tea
For a cup of soothing tea, use a teaspoon of fresh Catnip. For a pot, use a handful. Steep in boiling water at least 10 minutes, covered.

"What Cramps?" Cocktail
2 oz. organic wine (ask for one with no sulfites)
1C fresh Catnip tea (or one dropperful fresh Catnip tincture)

Prepare a strong tea by pouring a cup of boiling water over a small handful of fresh Catnip. Pour the wine into a glass. Strain 2 oz. of the tea into the wine. Sip slowly. Refrigerate leftover tea for later use. This remedy will probably make you very sleepy. Don't drive, work, or try to do anything other than serve your own needs at this time.

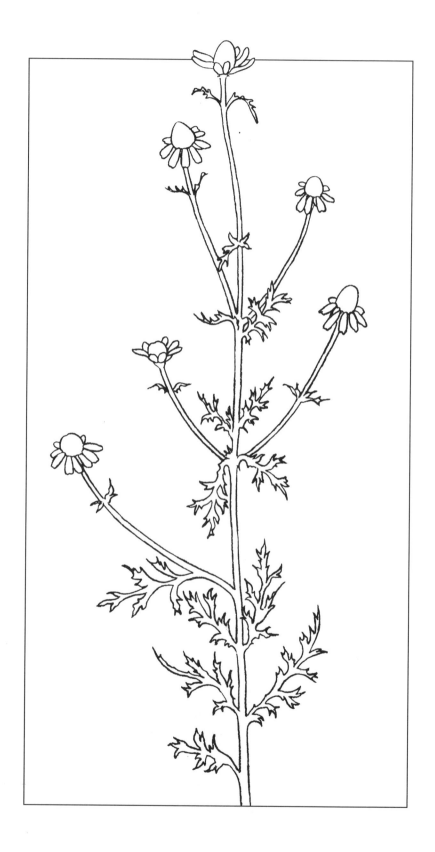

Chamomile

Matricaria recutita, Ground Apple

Soothing, mineral-rich Chamomile is especially high in calcium, with a wide range of stress-reducing uses. The tea is mildly relaxing. The tincture helps those with stress symptoms related to irritability and insomnia. Chamomile also relaxes muscle spasms, making it particularly helpful for resolving digestive problems. Used externally, it makes a relaxing hot soak or headache remedy. The warmed oil infusion is wonderful for massage.

Uses
- Nourishes & strengthens nerves
- Promotes relaxation
- Eases tension headaches
- Soothes digestive upsets

Cultivation
Annual Chamomile starts easily from seed, but almost all weeds grow faster and stronger, so it takes some work to get a hearty bed going. Chamomile smells so delicious and comforting that weeding it is sweet medicine in itself. With lots of sun, Chamomile grows up to 20" tall and blooms in early summer, with some reflowering after each harvest until the frost. Harvest the flowers many at a time by using your fingers like a rake, palm up. The feathery green foliage is just as fragrant and useful as the little daisy-like flowers.

Preparation
Use only fresh for oil infusions. Use fresh or dried flowers and leaves for tea, tinctures, soaks, and steams. Brew with Lemon Balm for indigestion.

Chamomile/Lavender Headache Remedy
Put a handful each of fresh or dried Chamomile flowers and Lavender buds into a quart glass jar. Pour in boiling water to cover, steep for 20 minutes, and strain into a bowl. Soak a cotton wash cloth in the tea, wring out, fold, and cover forehead and eyes. Leave on til cool. Double the relief with a second cloth on the back of the neck. These herbs also make a soothing bath or steam facial.*

Chamomile Massage Oil **
Gather a large bunch of fresh flower heads. Spread on screens or newspapers to wilt overnight. Pack into a very dry glass quart jar. Pour in olive oil to cover the herb completely. Cap, label, and put it in a spot where you can easily check it every couple of days for mold. (Carefully lift any out with a spoon.) You will know your oil is ready to use when it smells strongly of herb — about two weeks. Strain the oil into a clean dry glass jar for storage. Cap, label, and date. To use, pour into a small plastic squeeze bottle. Use freely for massage.

*More about herbal baths and steam facials on page 24. **More about oil infusions on page 22.

Lavender

Lavendula augustifolia, English Lavender "Munstead"

Lavender's unmistakable, relaxing aroma may be the most familiar herbal fragrance of all. Used for centuries, it has never gone out of favor as a gentle sedative and muscle relaxer. It also works as a painkiller, antidepressant, and tonic strengthener for the whole nervous system, especially useful when grief interferes with sleep. To soothe stress and help you cope, turn to Lavender.

Uses
- Nourishes & strengthens nerves
- Lifts depression
- Lowers blood pressure
- Eases tension headaches
- Soothes irritability
- Induces restful sleep without hangover

Cultivation
Sow Munstead outside in a sunny, sandy, limy spot in late fall for germination the following spring. It grows up to 18" and is hardy to below 0°F if well-drained, mulched, and protected from wind. Otherwise, pot it up to overwinter inside. Once established, it has woody stems, grey-green leaves, and lavender colored flowers. Blooms in early summer beginning the second year. Harvest just before the flower buds begin to open. Snip stems a handslength up from the ground, tie in small bunches (2-4 stems), and hang upside down out of direct sun to dry.

Preparation
Use dried buds for tea and baths. Lavender works well with Skullcap to lift depression, and with Valerian or Chamomile to relieve pain of tension headaches.

Lavender Shortbread
1/2 lb. (2 sticks) unsalted organic butter	Pinch of salt
1 C rice flour (white or brown)	1 C unbleached all-purpose flour
1/4 C (scant) Demerara (unprocessed) sugar	1T dried Lavender buds

Cream butter and sugar. Add flours, salt, and Lavender, mix well. Divide dough in half and pat into 2 ungreased pie pans. Score the dough for 12 slices and prick all over with a fork. Bake at 300° for 40-50 minutes, until cooked but not brown. Let cool, then slice through. Store in an airtight tin. Keeps well.

Lavender Salt Glow *
Grind 1 cup dried Lavender buds in a blender or food processor. Add 3 cups Epsom salts, grind until fine. Store in a glass jar, tightly capped. To use, rinse yourself off in the shower, then turn water off. Pour a handful of bath salts into your palm, and massage gently into your skin all over your body (not your face). Use more as needed. Rinse off, towel dry lightly, and moisturize.

* More about salt glows on page 24.

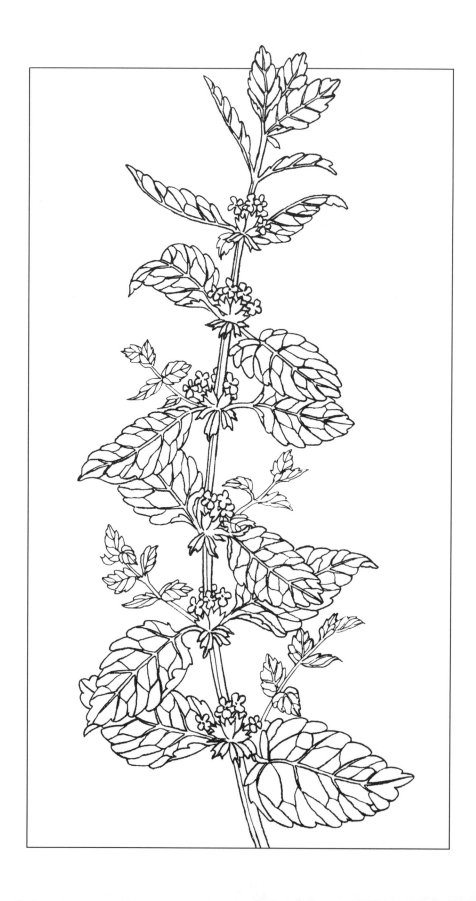

Lemon Balm

Melissa officinalis, Balm

Lemon Balm is a favorite serenity herb worldwide. It combines a mild sedative action on the nerves with a mild stimulant action on circulation and digestion. Lemon Balm tea tastes delicious and makes an excellent daily tonic, said to strengthen the heart and promote long life. It also has antiviral properties that relieve the general stress of any illness. Lemon Balm tea provides quick relief for flu sufferers. Applied externally, Lemon Balm salve shortens the course of herpes outbreaks. Safe for long-term use, even for children.

Uses
- Nourishes & strengthens nerves
- Calms anxiety, promotes relaxation
- Lifts depression
- Eases tension & migraine headaches
- Tones heart, lowers blood pressure
- Stimulates digestion

Cultivation
Lemon Balm is easy to grow from seed started outside in spring. It will do fine in sun or light shade, but good loamy soil is a must. Lemon Balm grows up to 3' tall, with lemon-scented leaves and small white flowers that bloom in mid- to late summer. Harvest the top third of the plant anytime up until flowering begins. Leave a few blossoms to self-sow. Cover with leaves or hay after the ground freezes.

Preparation
Eat the fresh leaves. Use fresh or dried leaves for tea. Cover while steeping to preserve volatile oils. Lemon Balm works well with Chamomile to soothe your upset stomach, and with Lavender to a ease tension headache.

Lemon Balm Sun Tea
Put two handfuls of fresh Lemon Balm leaves (or a handful of dried) into a clear glass quart jar. Pour in cold water to fill, cover, and put the jar in a sunny spot (inside or out) to steep for an hour or more. Strain and serve straight or over ice.

Lemon Balm Salve *
1 cup Lemon Balm oil infusion   2T grated beeswax

Begin by making an oil infusion of fresh Lemon Balm as the base for your salve. See page 22 for directions. Strain 1 cup of the oil into a saucepan. Over very low heat, add the wax to the oil and stir until melted. Drop some onto a plate. If drop is too stiff, add more oil. If too runny, add more grated wax. Remove pan from heat. Continue stirring until the salve starts to set up, then pour into small wide-mouth glass jars for storage at room temperature. Keeps for several years. Use topically as needed to reduce pain and duration of herpes outbreaks.

* More about salves on page 25.

Skullcap

Scutellaria lateriflora, Helmet Flower

Used worldwide as a safe, nourishing nervine, Skullcap is strong enough when tinctured fresh to be useful for dealing with nervous exhaustion, migraines, anxiety attacks, and even seizures. As a tea, it is mild enough for children to use on a daily basis. An effective pain reliever, Skullcap also alleviates irritability, depression, and PMS/menstrual symptoms. It can reduce symptoms of withdrawal from alcohol or barbiturates. Tonic Skullcap is very high in copper, necessary for energy conduction, and in zinc, potassium, and vitamin C, all vital nutrients for cell repair, nerve function and balanced metabolism.

Uses
- Nourishes & strengthens nerves
- Eases migraine headaches
- Calms anxiety
- Reduces irritability & cravings of withdrawal
- Induces restful sleep without hangover
- Relieves pain, seizures

Cultivation

A North American native, Skullcap is a perennial Mint that does best in moist, lightly-shaded areas like the edge of a woods or the back of a shady border. Wild populations are in danger of extinction. Seeds need stratification — 7 days of cold storage — before they will germinate. (See page 19 for directions.) Once established outside, spindly Skullcap can grow up to 3' tall, but often has a habit of lying down and sending up smaller side shoots. It blooms in late summer with small blue-purple flowers. Harvest the top third of the plant (flowers, leaves, and stems) in full bloom.

Preparation

Use fresh when possible, especially for tinctures. Tone the nerves with 1-2 cups of tea per day. For acute symptoms, take 2-3 droppersful of tincture. Larger or more frequent doses are not recommended. Skullcap works well with Valerian for pain relief.

Skullcap Nightcap
Make one cup of Chamomile, Lemon Balm or Lavender tea. Add one dropperful of fresh Skullcap tincture. Enjoy at bedtime.

Serene Dream Pillow
Dry and mix together your favorite radical weeds from Serenity Garden. Carefully remove all stems. Stuff a small pillow case (or a muslin tea bag or a sock or an old shirt pocket) and stitch it securely closed. Place your head on your pillow and dream on! To add soothing heat and increase the aroma, toss the pillow in the dryer for a few minutes first.

Valerian

Valerianus officialis, All-heal

Valerian root was perhaps the most widely used herbal anesthetic and sedative in western cultures until the invention of morphine. At lower doses it acts as a nervine; at higher doses as a pain killer. Its powerful action also lowers blood pressure, and it can be used to take the edge off extreme pain, anxiety, or grief. Because Valerian is a central nervous system depressant, it is primarily used as a situational remedy rather than a daily tonic. Don't drive a car or use power tools while taking Valerian.

Uses
- Allays acute anxiety & emotional distress
- Relieves severe pain
- Eases migraine headaches
- Lowers blood pressure

Cultivation
Sow the seed outside in spring. Roots spread easily after they're well established. Valerian will tolerate partial sun but really loves shade, and rich, loose soil with lots of organic manure. Blooms in spring with clusters of delicate white flowers on tall stalks (18-24"), and a very distinctive fragrance. Harvest the pungent, spidery roots in fall after the foliage has died back, or in early spring before the flower stalk comes up. Roots are ready for harvest after the second year. Cats love strong smelling Valerian as much as Catnip, and they will often appear to help you harvest it.

Preparation
Use fresh roots for tinctures and cleaned, dried, ground roots for capsules. The fresh root makes a stronger remedy. Alternate with Skullcap for longterm use. Do not use for more than 2 weeks daily or 6 weeks in alternation with Skullcap. NOTE: Some people are stimulated rather than sedated by Valerian. Start with a low dose of the tincture (15-20 drops) and monitor the effects.

Valerian Tincture
Fill a clean glass jar to the top with fresh Valerian root. Cover with vodka or all-natural brandy, cap, label and date. Decant in six weeks by straining into dark glass dropper bottles.

Valerian Caps *
Finely grind two handfuls of chopped, dried Valerian root in a coffee grinder or food processor. Transfer the powder to a glass bowl. Wash and dry your hands, then fill and cap clear size 1 vegetable gelatin capsules. Store the filled capsules in a dark glass jar with a tight cover. Label, date, and store away from heat. Take 1-2 capsules with one cup of hot water 1-3 times daily before meals.

* More about capsules on page 25.

Starting Seeds Indoors & Out

Your postcard for seven free seed packets is on page 27. You'll find all the specific instructions needed to cultivate your seeds on the back of each seed packet. Also, be sure to refer to the cultivation information on the page for each plant in this book. For more about propagating seeds and cultivating weeds, check the list of Additional Resources on page 26.

STARTING SEEDS INDOORS:

Start with a sterile potting mix of about 80% peat (to hold moisture) and 20% perlite (for drainage). Add a little water to the mix and stir it up with your hands until it's soft and fluffy. Scoop the mix into a seedling tray (or a paper cup or an egg carton — you can use anything you can poke a hole in for bottom drainage), scrape off the excess, and tamp down. Shake the seed out carefully. Don't sow too thickly, as it will stunt seedling growth and make it difficult to separate and transplant later on. The rule of thumb is to plant seeds about twice as deep as they are long.

Make a label for each different variety of seed. (You can buy markers at a nursery, or use popsicle sticks.) Cover the seeds with a layer of vermiculite for water retention and protection. Place on a tray in a warm spot with bright but not direct light, and water thoroughly with warm water, preferably using a mister. Keep the growing mixture moist until the seeds sprout. To avoid rot, water only in the morning. If your house is dry, use a humidity dome (or a plastic bag with a few holes poked in it) over the seed tray. Take it off as soon as seedlings appear, or they'll get too leggy.

Seedlings usually appear in 7-21 days, but sometimes take longer, depending on the variety. Whenever they come up, they'll continue to need lots of light but not so much heat or water. For strong stem development, it's best to keep them on the dryish side. Water from the bottom as needed. When the first real leaves appear, begin to feed weekly with a half-strength solution of water-soluble, organic fertilizer that will provide an even ratio (20-20-20) of nitrogen for growth, phosphorus for flowers and roots, and potash for strong stems.

When the seedlings have two sets of real leaves, you can transplant them: first to small pots and then, when they're about 6 inches high, outside. Before transplanting seedlings to your garden, harden them off for a week or so by putting them outside during the day and bringing them inside to an unheated garage or porch at night.

Starting seeds outdoors:

This method is called "direct seeding." Wait until all danger of frost is past. Rake thoroughly to break up the soil surface. Mix seeds with a little sand for a more even broadcast when you sow. Scatter seeds in the loose dirt, then rake again to cover lightly. Keep the area uniformly moist until seeds sprout. Water regularly until seedlings are well-established — about six weeks. Thereafter, water and feed as necessary.

Special seed treatments: soaking, scarification, stratification

Whether you sow your seeds indoors or out, pre-treating any hard-coated seeds will help them to germinate. Soaking is the easiest treatment method. Cover seeds with warm water and soak for 24 hours. Most of them will expand several sizes during this period. (Those that don't may not germinate, but try planting them, anyway.) Sow immediately; don't let the seeds dry out. Some hard-coated seeds need to be scarified before soaking and sowing, in order to allow water through their tough coats. Scarification is the process of gently nicking or filing the seed coat in one small spot — you can use the tip or rasp of a metal nail file to do this.

Other dormant seeds require stratification — a period of damp, cold storage — before planting. Sow these seeds in a seed tray (described in starting seed indoors). Barely cover seeds, and make sure soil mixture is moist. Put the whole thing in a large plastic bag and close the end with a knot or a twist tie. Refrigerate for a period of a few days up to six weeks, depending on the plant. After this cold treatment, transfer the seed tray to a warmer, brighter spot to germinate. Remove the plastic bag as soon as seedlings appear, and feed and transplant according to directions on page 18. To stratify seed for direct seeding, store unopened packets in the freezer for the specified time before sowing outdoors.

Germination and maturation

Most of the plants in Serenity Garden are perennials. Once they are established in your garden, they will come back for many years with very little effort on your part. Catnip, Skullcap, and Lemon Balm are shorter-lived perennials that will need replacement or transplanting every 2-3 years. Longer-lived perennials mature more slowly, so you won't be able to dig Valerian roots, for example, or harvest Lavender flowers, until their second or third years.

California Poppy and German Chamomile are annuals which will mature quickly and may self-sow, especially in warmer areas. With care and good growing conditions, you'll be able to use them within a few months of sowing the seeds.

This chart outlines the preferred sowing method and approximate times to germination and harvest for each of the seven radical weeds in Serenity Garden. While your garden grows, you can make many of the remedies in this book (teas, water infusions, salt glows, baths, capsules) using dried organic herbs. Commercially made fresh plant tinctures are also readily available. (See page 26.)

Plant	Sowing Method	Approx. Time to Germination	Approx. Time to Useful Stage of Growth
California Poppy	direct seed in spring	1-2 weeks	2-3 months to flowers, leaves & roots
Catnip	direct seed in spring	1-2 weeks	2 months to leaves
Chamomile	direct seed in spring	1-2 weeks	2-3 months to flowers & leaves
Lavender	direct seed in fall	8-9 months	1-2 years to flowers
Lemon Balm	direct seed in spring	1-2 weeks	2 months to leaves
Skullcap	stratify seed 7 days in spring	1-2 weeks	3 months to flowers & leaves
Valerian	direct seed in spring	1-3 weeks	2 years to roots

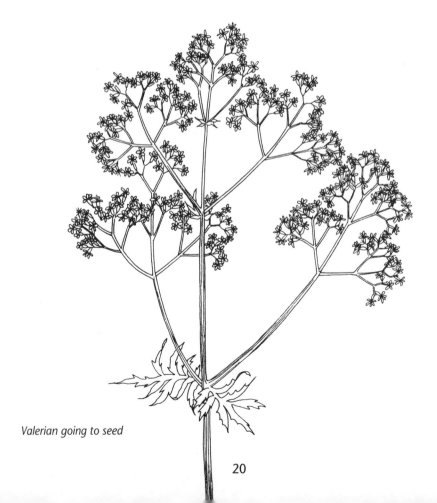

Valerian going to seed

Harvesting & Storing Plants & Seeds

Flowers & Leaves

If you're harvesting plant material to dry, or to use in an oil infusion, be sure to pick when the plants are dry to begin with. If you're harvesting to make a tincture or water infusion right away, you can pick in the rain, but you won't get the full strength of the plant. The best time to pick, no matter what you plan to do with the harvest, is in the morning on a sunny day, as soon as all the dew is dry. This is when the plant's essential oils will be at their peak strength. Whenever you pick, always leave some plants behind to go to seed.

If you don't plan to use your harvest right away, tie bunches of stems together and hang upside down, or spread on screens or newspaper, in a dry, cool, dark room. Drying time depends on the weather and the plant part. It can take two days to two weeks. Plants are dry when the thickest part snaps or crunches to touch. Store in brown paper bags, labelled with name and date, in a cool, dry place. Under these storage conditions, potency lasts at least a year.

It's not necessary to strip leaves and flowers from stems before storage. In fact, breaking the plant down this way will increase oxidation, which will release the plant's stored energy much more quickly. To maintain freshness and potency, store your dried herbs whole, and crush or powder them only at point of use.

Roots

The usual time to harvest roots is in the fall, after the plant has flowered and gone to seed. You can also harvest roots in early spring, before they send up stalks. Dig roots out carefully, and sever with sharp trowel, knife, or hand-ax. Use a small brush like a toothbrush to remove all dirt, chop into small pieces, and use fresh if indicated. Dry chopped roots on a screen or newspaper out of direct light in a cool, dry place. Store in brown paper bags, labelled and dated. Dried roots retain potency for years.

Seeds

Most herb seeds are easily gathered by hand after flower petals have fallen away and stems have begun to dry. Alternatively, you can cut bunches of dried stems and hang them upside down in paper bags. The seeds will eventually fall into the bags and you can retrieve them for storage. Whichever gathering method you use, most of your seeds should remain viable for a couple of years if you store them in a dry, cool place. Many garden supply stores sell blank seed packets, or you can use your own envelopes. Label, date, and put away in a dry cupboard for the seasons to come.

Making Plant Remedies

A weed can go from being a simple food to a daily tonic to a potent medicine, depending on how it's prepared and taken. No matter what the preparation, the general dosing guide that we use for herbal remedies is two weeks on followed by two weeks off. This gentle approach allows you to evaluate a remedy's effects and adjust the dosage (frequency and amount) as necessary according to how you feel.

TEAS

A tea is a quick brew, generally of leaf and flower, made by pouring boiling water over an herb and steeping for ten minutes to half an hour. We suggest crushing or bruising the whole herb at the time of preparation to ensure freshness and potency. The usual proportions are one teaspoon of dried herb to one cup of tea; one handful to a pot of tea. If you use fresh ingredients, just double the amount. You can use a muslin or one-use tea bag or other tea steeper if you like. Teas are nutritious fare. Taken over a long period, teas can slowly build health and strength by nourishing many body systems at once. A daily pot of Lemon Balm tea, for example, has a tonic effect on the whole body over time.

WATER INFUSIONS

A water infusion is a very strong tea, steeped over 8-12 hours, which generally amps up the effect of an herb from tonic to medicinal. To make a water infusion, add two handfuls of dried herb (roughly an ounce) to a quart mason jar, pour in boiling water to the brim, and cover for the day or night. Strain, and refrigerate what you don't use. You can reheat water infusions, and they generally stay fresh up to three days under refrigeration. The usual dose is 1 cup morning and night, but directions vary with each plant. Many water infusions can also be used topically -- to clean wounds, for example, or as compresses.

OIL INFUSIONS

Oil infusions need care and attention. If any water gets into an oil infusion, it will be spoiled by mold. Harvest the top third of the flowering plant and spread it on a screen or newspaper to wilt overnight. This will drop the moisture content and give the bugs a chance to get away. The next day, start by drying a clean quart glass jar in a 200-degree oven for five minutes. (Even if your jar appears dry at the outset, the oven will evaporate extra moisture.)

Bruise and break up the plant, pack it loosely into the oven-dried jar, and fill the jar with olive oil. Use a wooden spoon to stir out any air bubbles, which can cause the mixture to spoil. Make sure the plant material is completely submerged in oil, then cap, label and date. Store on a saucer to catch overflow in case gas bubbles form. Check the infusion daily for signs of mold, and use a spoon to lift off any small bits carefully so as not to spread it.

Two weeks is usually plenty of time to steep the mixture. The nose knows. When the infusion smells strongly of herb, it is ready to decant. Line a sieve with cheesecloth to strain the oil through a funnel into dry, wide-mouthed glass bottles or jars for storage. Don't squeeze the plant while you strain, or you will add water to the oil. If this happens, strain the oil into a measuring cup and let it sit overnight. You can then pour the oil into your storage jars, leaving any water behind. Strained, bottled oil infusions can be stored up to two years at room temperature because olive oil itself is a natural preservative. Use a small plastic squeeze bottle to dispense.

TINCTURES

A tincture is a plant extract made by using alcohol as a solvent to pull the plant's healing properties into solution. In this form, the remedy is readily absorbed directly through the lining of the mouth and stomach. An all-natural brandy makes an excellent solvent. So does vodka. Tinctures made with either one require no refrigeration and have a shelf life of at least 5 years. If you use brandy, we recommend E & J brand, which has no additives or preservatives and is 40% alcohol (80 proof). If you use vodka, any 80 proof brand will do. Stronger alcohol content is unnecessary. Wine is sometimes used for leaf and flower tinctures. These will keep up to a year in the refrigerator. Ask at your health food store or wine shop for a sulfite-free brand.

Anyone concerned about alcohol consumption can evaporate the alcohol in a dose of tincture by putting the dose into a coffee cup and pouring a small amount (about 1/4 cup) of boiling water over it. Cool and drink.

Tincture recipes generally call for fresh plant material and specify which plant part/s to use. Roughly chop enough plants to fill a glass jar, and pour in alcohol to cover. Cap, label, and place on a saucer in case of leaks. Decant after six weeks by straining through cheesecloth or a sieve into a clean glass jar or measuring cup. Pour into dark glass dropper bottles, label, date and store. An adult dose varies according to the specific plant. A dose is usually taken under the tongue and held in the mouth for several seconds before swallowing, but it can also be taken in a small amount of water.

To maximize the energy extraction process, put up your tinctures with the new or waxing moon and decant them six weeks later with the full moon of the next cycle.

Herbal Baths

Nothing soothes frazzled nerves like a long soak in warm water. Adding aromatic and soothing herbs to your bath maximizes the benefits of hydrotherapy. Dried Chamomile and Lavender flowers, Lemon Balm leaves, and Valerian root, used singly or in combination, make excellent bath herbs. You can also use Roses, Rosemary, Calendula...or whatever appeals to you.

For a bath sachet, fill a muslin drawstring tea bag (or a cotton sock) with dried herb/s. Hang the bag from the faucet as you fill the tub. When tub is full, take the bag off the faucet and let it float, squeezing it occasionally to release the aroma. You can also use the bag/sock as an herbal body scrub in bath or shower.

You may prefer to add strained herbal teas to your tub or footbath. Add a generous handful of dried herb/s to a quart jar. Fill the jar with boiling water, cover, and let steep at least 20 minutes. Strain, pour into bath water, swirl to disperse.

Steam Facials

Enjoy the soothing, aromatic properties of your herbs by treating yourself to a steam facial. Use a handful of sweet-smelling herbs like Chamomile, Lavender, or Lemon Balm. Place in a large bowl and cover with boiling water. Position yourself high enough above the bowl so that you can inhale the herbal steam comfortably and deeply, without burning. Drape your head and shoulders with a bath towel to trap the steam, and adjust your position as necessary for comfort. This relaxing treatment tones the face, soothes the body, and quiets the mind.

Salt Glows

We build up about a quarter pound of dandruff all over our bodies in the course of a week. A weekly salt glow (complete rubdown/massage with Epsom salts followed by a warm water rinse) is ideal for exfoliating skin and renewing spirits. Enhance the treatment by mixing bath herbs with the Epsom salts. Use one cup of herb/s to three cups of Epsom salts. First grind the herb/s in a food processor or coffee mill. Add the Epsom salts and continue grinding until very fine, with no plant material large enough to clog the drain.

You can give yourself (or a partner) a salt glow in the shower or standing in a bath tub. First rinse off with warm water, then massage handfuls of herbal bath salts gently into the skin all over the body (except head and face). Rinse yourself again with warm water (no soap!), towel dry lightly, and while you're still a little damp, massage in your favorite moisturizer from top to toes.

Salves

To make a healing topical salve, start with a base of olive oil infused with the fresh flowering herb of your choice. (Making an herbal oil infusion takes about 2 weeks. See page 22 for directions.) You'll also need pure beeswax, which you can usually find at natural foods stores. To make a smooth mixture, it will take at least two tablespoons of grated beeswax for every cup of infused oil that you use.

Strain the oil into a saucepan. Grate the beeswax. Add the wax to the oil and stir with a wooden spoon over very low heat until all the wax has melted. To test consistency, drop a little onto a plate. If it's too stiff, add more oil. If it's too runny, add more grated wax. Remove pan from heat. Continue stirring until the salve cools and starts to set up, then pour into small wide-mouth glass jars. Label, date, and store at room temperature, away from heat. Keeps for at least two years.

Capsules

If you prefer your remedy in pill form, you can purchase plain gelatin capsules at any health food store. To get your dried plant materials finely ground, use a mortar and pestle for small amounts, or a spice or coffee grinder for larger jobs. Transfer powdered material to a bowl. Wash and dry hands, then fill gelatin capsules with powder and close. Label and store in tightly closed dark glass jars. Capsules are most effective when taken just before a meal with a glass of hot water. This will melt the gelatin, releasing the herbs for digestion. The usual dose is 1-2 capsules 1-3 times daily before meals for up to two weeks.

Additional Resources

Recommended books about stress and weeds:

AN HERBAL GUIDE TO STRESS RELIEF
by David Hoffmann
Healing Arts Press, c 1986, 1987, 1991

STRESS & NATURAL HEALING
by Christopher Hobbs
Interweave Press, Inc., 1997

HERBS FOR HEALTH AND HEALING
by Kathi Keville with Peter Korn
Berkeley Press, 1996

Recommended books about propagation, cultivation, & identification:

RODALE'S ILLUSTRATED ENCYCLOPEDIA OF HERBS
Claire Kowalchik & William H. Hylton, eds.
Rodale Press, 1987

PARK'S SUCCESS WITH SEEDS
by Ann Reilly
Geo. W. Park Seed Co., Inc., 1978

PARK'S SUCCESS WITH HERBS
by Gertrude B. Foster and Rosemary F. Louden
Geo. W. Park Seed Co., Inc., 1980

MAGIC AND MEDICINE OF PLANTS
Inge N. Dobelis, ed.
Reader's Digest, 1986

Recommended supplier

RADICAL REMEDIES
321 Anawan
Rehoboth, MA 02769

jilweed@aol.com

One-stop source for dried organic herbs, freshly-made remedies, and supplies like dropper bottles, tea bags, gel caps, and beeswax. Owned and operated by coauthor Jillian VanNostrand. Free brochure.

TO GET YOUR FREE, FRESH SEEDS

Your seeds will come from **Johnny's Selected Seeds** in Albion, ME. If any seed is unavailable, Johnny's reserves the right to substitute another from this garden, or a comparable variety. Johnny's will send seeds ONLY upon receipt of this ORIGINAL postcard.
Mail when you're ready to plant.

TO GET ANOTHER COPY OF THIS BOOK
(or any other book in this series)

Send check or money order for $11 per book + $4 s/h (+ $.50 s/h for each additional book) to
Radical Weeds, P.O. Box 68, Mirror Lake, NH 03853.
Credit card orders call toll-free 1-888-697-WEED. Order online at www.radicalweeds.com.

SERENITY GARDEN

TO: **JOHNNY'S SELECTED SEEDS**: Order Fulfillment

Please send 1 packet of each of these 7 seeds to the gardener listed below.

CALIFORNIA POPPY, CATNIP, CHAMOMILE, LAVENDER, LEMON BALM, SKULLCAP, VALERIAN

SHIP TO:

NAME:_____

STREET ADDRESS:_____

MAILING ADDRESS:_____

TOWN:_____ STATE:_____

ZIP:_____ PHONE:_____

TO: **RADICAL WEEDS / SERENITY GARDEN**

❏ PLEASE ADD ME TO YOUR MAILING LIST.
❏ PLEASE SEND ME A RADICAL REMEDIES BROCHURE

NAME:_____

MAILING ADDRESS:_____

_____ZIP:_____

E-MAIL ADDRESS:_____

❏ PLEASE ADD MY RADICAL FRIEND TO YOUR MAILING LIST.

NAME:_____

ADDRESS:_____

_____ZIP:_____

 SERENITY GARDEN

Place Postcard Stamp Here

Johnny's Selected Seeds
Introductory Packet 8001
Department 840
RR 1   Box 2580
Albion, ME   04910-9731

Place Postcard Stamp Here

RADICAL WEEDS
P.O. Box 68
Mirror Lake, NH   03853-0068